P9-CBB-134

J
567.9
DIX

CERATOSAURUS
AND OTHER FIERCE DINOSAURS

by **Dougal Dixon**

illustrated by
Steve Weston and **James Field**

PICTURE WINDOW BOOKS
Minneapolis, Minnesota

CALUMET CITY PUBLIC LIBRARY

Picture Window Books
5115 Excelsior Boulevard
Suite 232
Minneapolis, MN 55416
877-845-8392
www.picturewindowbooks.com

Copyright © 2006 by Picture Window Books
All rights reserved. No part of this book may be
reproduced without written permission from the
publisher. The publisher takes no responsibility
for the use of any of the materials or methods
described in this book, nor for the products thereof.

Printed in the United States of America.

Library of Congress Cataloging-in-Publication Data
Dixon, Dougal.
Ceratosaurus and other fierce dinosaurs / by Dougal
Dixon ; illustrated by Steve Weston & James Field.
p. cm. – (Dinosaur find)
Includes bibliographical references and index.
ISBN 1-4048-1327-6
1. Dinosaurs—Behavior—Juvenile literature.
2. Ceratosaurus—Behavior—Juvenile literature.
3. Carnivora, Fossil—Juvenile literature. I. Weston,
Steve, ill. II. Field, James, 1959- ill. III. Title.
QE861.6.B44D59 2006
567.912—dc22   2005023334

Acknowledgments
This book was produced for Picture Window Books by
Bender Richardson White, U.K.

Illustrations by James Field (pages 4–5, 11, 13,
19, 21) and Steve Weston (cover and pages 7,
9, 15, 17).
Diagrams by Stefan Chabluk.
All photographs copyright Digital Vision.

Consultant: John Stidworthy, Scientific Fellow of
the Zoological Society, London, and former
Lecturer in the Education Department, Natural
History Museum, London.

Reading Adviser: Susan Kesselring, M.A., Literacy
Educator, Rosemount-Apple Valley-Eagan
(Minnesota) School District

Types of dinosaurs

In this book, a red shape at the top of a left-hand page shows the animal was a meat-eater. A green shape shows it was a plant-eater.

Just how big—or small— were they?

Dinosaurs were many different sizes. We have compared their sizes to one of the following:

Chicken
2 feet (60 centimeters) tall
6 pounds (2.7 kilograms)

Adult person
6 feet (1.8 meters) tall
170 pounds (76.5 kg)

Elephant
10 feet (3 m) tall
12,000 pounds
(5,400 kg)

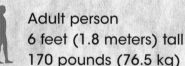

Table of Contents

What's Inside?

Dinosaurs lived between 230 and 65 million years ago. These dinosaurs were some of the fiercest. Find out how they lived and what they have in common with today's animals.

THE FIERCEST DINOSAURS

The Age of Dinosaurs was a fearsome time. Dinosaurs were some of the fiercest animals ever to have lived. They killed and ate smaller animals and other dinosaurs. Even after they had killed their prey, the meat-eaters then had to fend off scavengers.

A dead *Iguanodon* lay by the side of a swamp as two *Baryonyx* ate it. A *Neovenator* prowled around, trying to feed on the *Iguanodon*, too.

TYRANNOSAURUS

Pronunciation:
tie-RAN-uh-SAW-rus

The largest and fiercest meat-eating dinosaur at the end of the Age of Dinosaurs was *Tyrannosaurus*. It must have hunted and eaten the biggest plant-eaters of its day. Its mouth was big enough to have swallowed you in one gulp.

Big killer today

The polar bear is the biggest and fiercest hunter of its homeland, just like the *Tyrannosaurus* was.

Size Comparison

Tyrannosaurus had teeth that were the size of bananas. The teeth were strong enough to plunge into and hold an animal as big as an elephant.

UTAHRAPTOR

Pronunciation:
YOU-tah-RAP-tur

The hands of *Utahraptor* were like massive meat hooks. The dinosaur used the huge claws on its feet to rip out the insides of the biggest animals around. With its jaws, it tore at the flesh of its victims. No animal wanted to get too close to this dinosaur.

Hunting in packs today

Cheetahs often hunt in packs like *Utahraptor* did long ago.

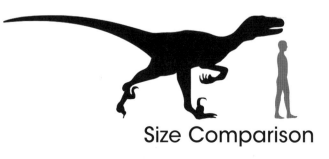

Size Comparison

Utahraptor usually attacked and killed plant-eaters that were too slow to run away or could not defend themselves.

VELOCIRAPTOR

Pronunciation:
veh-LAW-sih-RAP-tur

Velociraptor was small but very fierce. It could fight and kill the well-protected horned dinosaurs that lived at that time. Its jagged teeth were as sharp as steak knives.

Feathered killer today

The golden eagle is a feathered hunter that kills its prey by tearing it apart. *Velociraptor* was feathered, too, and killed in the same way.

Size Comparison

Velociraptor could stand on one foot and slash at its prey with the big claw on the other foot. Its long tail helped it stay balanced.

CALUMET CITY PUBLIC LIBRARY

11

Neovenator prowled through the swamps, looking for other animals to eat. It was big and fast-moving. With its sharp claws and pointed teeth, it could eat both slow-moving large animals and fast-moving small ones.

Water-hunter today

Tigers often go into rivers and swamps to catch animals like *Neovenator* did millions of years before.

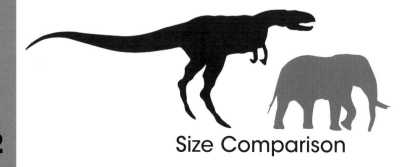

Size Comparison

A *Neovenator* could wade through shallow water, hunting and killing the other animals that had come to drink.

DEINONYCHUS

Deinonychus was tiny, fierce, and fast. It was harder to escape from a *Deinonychus* than from a *Tyrannosaurus*. When it hunted in packs, *Deinonychus* was probably the most fearsome of all dinosaurs.

Teeth and claws today

A hyena uses its teeth and claws to kill and tear apart its prey like *Deinonychus* did.

Size Comparison

A pack of *Deinonychus* surrounded a plant-eating dinosaur. As they got closer to their victim, they spread out and attacked from all sides.

CERATOSAURUS

Pronunciation:
si-RAT-uh-SAW-rus

When *Ceratosaurus* hunted the large plant-eaters, it usually left the healthy grown-ups alone. It looked for the defenseless youngsters or slow-moving elderly ones. These were the easiest to kill. It separated these animals from the herd, then attacked them.

The weakest links today

Lions chase herds of plant-eaters such as zebras, picking off the weakest animals like *Ceratosaurus* did.

Size Comparison

When chased by two *Ceratosaurus*, a baby *Apatosaurus* had no chance for survival. Its parents were unable to help.

BARYONYX

Pronunciation:
BAR-ee-ON-ix

With its long jaws and huge claws, *Baryonyx* was a fierce, fish-eating dinosaur. Often, it dipped its long snout into the water to grab fish. At other times, it hooked out fish with its claws.

Fish-eater today

Grizzly bears hunt fish in rivers, hooking them out with their claws and gripping them with their teeth like *Baryonyx* did millions of years before.

Size Comparison

Baryonyx was a menace to the fish that lived in the rivers of that time. It used its many small teeth to grab and hold its slippery prey.

19

DILONG

Pronunciation:
dye-LONG

Dilong lived along the edges of lakes and hunted small animals that lived there. It was about the size of a tiger and must have been just as fierce. All other animals would have been terrified of *Dilong*.

Lake-hunters today

Crocodiles hunt and kill animals that live close to lakes like *Dilong* once did.

Size Comparison

Little birds that wanted to feed along the edge of a lake would mob a *Dilong* that disturbed them.

21

WHERE DID THEY GO?

Dinosaurs are extinct, which means that none of them are alive today. Scientists study rocks and fossils to find clues about what happened to dinosaurs.

People have different explanations about what happened. Some people think a huge asteroid hit Earth and caused all sorts of climate changes, which caused the dinosaurs to die. Others think volcanic eruptions caused the climate to change and that killed the dinosaurs. No one knows for sure what happened to all the dinosaurs.

GLOSSARY

claws—tough, usually curved fingernails or toenails

flesh—the soft parts of an animal, especially the skin and muscles

herds—large groups of animals that move, feed, and sleep together

horns—pointed structures on the head

packs—groups of animals that hunt and kill together

prey—animals that are hunted by other animals for food

prowl—to move slowly and silently

scavengers—animals that wanted to steal prey from other animals and eat it themselves

snout—a long, sticking-out nose

swamp—wet, spongy ground thick with plants

TO LEARN MORE

AT THE LIBRARY

Clark, Neil, and William Lindsay. *1001 Facts About Dinosaurs.* New York: Backpack Books, Dorling Kindersley, 2002.

Dixon, Dougal. *Dougal Dixon's Amazing Dinosaurs.* Honesdale, Penn.: Boyds Mills Press, 2000.

Holtz, Thomas, and Michael Brett-Surman. *Jurassic Park Institute Dinosaur Field Guide.* New York: Random House, 2001.

ON THE WEB

FactHound offers a safe, fun way to find Internet sites related to this book. All of the sites on FactHound have been researched by our staff.

1. Visit *www.facthound.com*
2. Type in this special code for age-appropriate sites: 1404813276
3. Click on the FETCH IT button.

Your trusty FactHound will fetch the best sites for you!

LOOK FOR ALL OF THE BOOKS IN THE DINOSAUR FIND SERIES:

Ankylosaurus and Other Mountain Dinosaurs 1-4048-0670-9
Centrosaurus and Other Dinosaurs of Cold Places 1-4048-0672-5
Ceratosaurus and Other Fierce Dinosaurs 1-4048-1327-6
Deltadromeus and Other Shoreline Dinosaurs 1-4048-0669-5
Giganotosaurus and Other Big Dinosaurs 1-4048-1325-X
Ornithomimus and Other Fast Dinosaurs 1-4048-1326-8

Plateosaurus and Other Desert Dinosaurs 1-4048-0667-9
Saltopus and Other First Dinosaurs 1-4048-1328-4
Scutellosaurus and Other Small Dinosaurs 1-4048-1330-6
Stegosaurus and Other Plains Dinosaurs 1-4048-0668-7
Styracosaurus and Other Last Dinosaurs 1-4048-1329-2
Triceratops and Other Forest Dinosaurs 1-4048-0671-7

INDEX